The Albert N'Yanza

[christmas summary classics]

(Sir Samuel Baker)

I.—*Explorations of the Nile Source*

Sir Samuel White Baker was born in London, on June 8, 1821. From early manhood he devoted himself to a life of adventure. After a year in Mauritius he founded a colony in the mountains of Ceylon at Newera Eliya, and later constructed the railway across the Dobrudsha. His discovery of the Albert N'yanza completed the labours of Speke and Grant, and solved the mystery of the Nile. Baker's administration of the Soudan was the first great effort to arrest the slave trade in the Nile Basin, and also the first step towards the establishment of the British Protectorate of Uganda and Somaliland. Baker died on December 30, 1893. He was a voluminous writer, and his books had immense popularity. "The Albert N'yanza" may be regarded as the most important of his works of travel by reason of the exploration which it records rather than on account of any exceptional literary merit. Here his story is one of such thrilling interest that even a dull writer could scarce have failed to hold the attention of any reader by its straightforward narration.

In March, 1861, I commenced an expedition to discover the sources of the Nile, with the hope of meeting the East African Expedition of Captains Speke and Grant that had been sent by the English Government from the south, via Zanzibar, for that object. From my youth I had been inured to hardships and endurance in wild sports in tropical climates; and when I gazed upon the map of Africa I had the hope that I might, by perseverance, reach the heart of Africa. Had I been alone it would have been no hard lot to die upon the untrodden path before me; but my wife resolved, with woman's constancy, to leave the luxuries of home and share all danger, and to follow me through each rough step in the wild life in which I was about to engage. Thus accompanied, on April 15, 1861, I sailed up the Nile from Cairo to Korosko; and thence, by a forced camel march across the Nubian desert, we reached the river of Abou Hamed, and, still on camels, though within view of the palm-trees that bordered the Nile, we came to Berber. I spent a year in learning Arabic, and while doing so explored the Atbara, which joins the Nile twenty miles south of Berber, and the Blue Nile, which joins the main stream at Khartoum, with all their affluents from the mountains of Abyssinia. The general result of these explorations was that I found that the waters of the Atbara when in flood are dense with soil washed from the fertile lands scoured by its tributaries after the melting of the snows and the rainy season; and these, joining with the Blue Nile in full flood, also charged with a red earthy matter, cause the annual inundation in Lower Egypt, the sediment from which gives to that country its remarkable fertility.

I reached Khartoum, the capital of the Soudan, on June 11, 1862. Moosa Pasha was at that time governor-general. He was a rather exaggerated specimen of Turkish authority, combining the worst of oriental failings with the brutality of the wild animal. At that time the Soudan was of little commercial importance to Egypt. What prompted the occupation of the country by the Egyptians was that the Soudan supplied slaves not only for Egypt, but for Arabia and Persia.

In the face of determined opposition of Moosa Pasha and the Nile traders, who were persuaded that my object in penetrating into unknown Central Africa was to put a stop to the nefarious slave traffic, I organised my expedition. It consisted of three vessels—a good decked diahbiah (for my wife, and myself and our personal attendants), and two noggurs, or sailing-barges—the latte to take stores, twenty-one donkeys, four camels and four horses. Forty-five armed men as escort, and forty sailors, all in brown uniform, with servants—ninety-six men in all—constituted my personnel.

On February 2, 1863, we reached Gondokoro, where I landed my animals and stores. It is a curious circumstance that, although many Europeans had been as far south as Gondokoro, I was the first Englishman who had ever reached it. Gondokoro I found a perfect hell. There were about 600 slave-hunters and ivory-traders and their people, who passed the whole of their time in drinking, quarrelling and ill-treating the slaves, of which the camps were full; and the natives assured me that there were large depots of slaves in the interior who would be marched to Gondokoro for shipment to the Soudan a few hours after my departure.

I had heard rumours of Speke and Grant, and determined to wait for a time before proceeding forward. Before very long there was a mutiny among my men, who wanted to make a "razzia" upon the cattle of the natives, which, of course, I prohibited. It had been instigated by the traders, who were determined, if possible, to stop my advance. With the heroic assistance of my wife, I quelled the revolt. On February 15, on the rattle of musketry at a great distance, my men rushed madly to my boat with the report that two white men, who had come from the sea, had arrived. Could they be Speke and Grant? Off I ran, and soon met them in reality; and, with a heart beating with joy, I took off my cap and gave a welcome hurrah! We were shortly seated on the deck of my diahbiah under the awning; and such rough fare as could be hastily prepared was set before these two ragged, careworn specimens of African travel. At the first blush of meeting them I considered my expedition as terminated, since they had discovered the Nile source; but upon my congratulating them with all my heart upon the honours they had so nobly earned, Speke and Grant, with characteristic generosity, gave me a map of their route, showing that they had been unable to complete the actual exploration of the Nile, and that the most important portion still remained to be determined. It appeared that in N. lat. 2° 17' they had crossed the Nile, which they had tracked from the Victoria Lake; but the river, which from its exit from that lake had a northern course, turned suddenly to the west from Karuma Falls (the point at which they crossed it at lat. 2° 17'). They did not see the Nile again until they arrived in N. lat. 3° 32', which was then flowing from the W.S.W. The natives and the King of Unyoro (Kamrasi) had assured them that the Nile from the Victoria N'yanza, which they had crossed at Karuma, flowed westward for several days' journey, and at length fell into a large lake called the Luta N'zige; that this lake came from the south, and that the Nile, on entering the northern extremity, almost immediately made its exit, and, as a navigable river, continued its course to the north, through the Koshi and Madi countries. Both Speke and Grant attached great importance to this lake Luta N'zige; and the former was much annoyed that it had been impossible for them to carry out the exploration.

I now heard that the field was not only open, but that an additional interest was given to the exploration by the proof that the Nile flowed out of one great lake, the Victoria, but that it evidently must derive an additional supply from an unknown lake as it entered it at the northern extremity, while the body of the lake came from the south. The fact of a great body of water, such as the Luta N'zige, extending in a direct line from south to north, while the general system of drainage of the Nile was from the same direction, showed most conclusively that the Luta N'zige, if it existed in the form assumed, must have an important position in the basin of the Nile. I determined, therefore, to go on. Speke and Grant, who were naturally anxious to reach England as soon as possible, sailed in my boat, on February 26, from Gondokoro for Khartoum. Our hearts were much too full to say more than a short "God bless you!" They had won their victory; my work lay all before me.

II.—Perils of Darkest Africa

My plan was to follow a party of traders known by the name of "Turks," and led by an Arab named Ibrahim, which was going to the Latooka country to trade for ivory and slaves, trusting to Providence, good fortune, and the virtue of presents. That party set out early in the afternoon of March 26, 1863. I had secured some rather unwilling men as drivers and porters, and was accompanied by two trusty followers, Richarn and a boy Saat, both of whom had been brought up in the Austrian mission in Khartoum. We had neither guide nor interpreter; but when the moon rose, knowing that the route lay on the east side of the mountain of Belignan, I led the way on my horse Filfil, Mrs. Baker riding by my side on my old Abyssinian hunter, Tétel, and the British flag following behind us as a guide for the caravan of heavily laden camels and donkeys. We pushed on over rough country intersected by ravines till we came to the valley of Tollogo, bounded with perpendicular walls of grey granite, one thousand feet in height, the natives of which were much excited at the sight of the horses and the camels, which were to them unknown animals. After passing through this defile, Ibrahim and his "Turks," whom we had passed during the previous night, overtook us. These slave-hunters and ivory-traders threatened effectually to spoil our enterprise, if not to secure the murder of Mrs. Baker, myself and my entire party, by raising the suspicion and enmity of the native tribes. We afterwards found that there had been a conspiracy to do this. We thought it best, therefore, to parley with Ibrahim, and came to terms with him by means of bribes of a double-barrelled gun and some gold.

Under his auspices our joint caravan cleared the palisaded villages of Ellyria, after paying blackmail to the chief, Leggé, whose villainous countenance was stamped with ferocity, avarice and sensuality. Glad to escape from this country, we crossed the

Kanīēti river, a tributary of the Sobat, itself a tributary of the White Nile, and entered the country of Latooka, which is bounded by the Lafeet chain of mountains. In the forests and on the plain were countless elephants, giraffes, buffaloes, rhinoceroses, and varieties of large antelopes, together with winged game. The natives are the finest savages I have ever seen, their average height being five feet eleven and a half inches, and their facial features remarkably pleasing. We stayed on many weeks at Tarrangollé, the capital, which is completely surrounded by palisaded walls, within which are over three thousand houses, each a little fort in itself, and kraals for twelve thousand head of cattle. In the neighbourhood I had some splendid big-game shooting; but we had difficulties with repeated mutinies of our men.

Early in May we left Latooka, and crossed a high mountain chain by a pass 2,500 feet in height into the beautiful country of Obbo. This is a fertile plateau, 3,674 feet above sea-level, with abundance of wild grapes and other fruits, yams, nuts, flax, tobacco, etc.; but the travelling was difficult owing to the high grass. The people are pleasant-featured and good-natured, and the chief, Katchiba, maintains his authority by a species of hocus-pocus, or sorcery. He is a merry soul, has a multiplicity of wives—a bevy in each village—so that when he travels through his kingdom he is always at home. His children number 116, and the government is quite a family affair, for he has one of his sons as chief in every village. A native of Obbo showed me some cowrie-shells which he said came from a country calledMagungo, situated on a lake so large that no one knew its limits. This lake, said I, can be no other than Luta N'zige which Speke had heard of, and I shall take the first opportunity to push for Magungo.

We returned to Latooka to pick up our stores and rejoin Ibrahim, but were detained by the illness of Mrs. Baker and myself and the loss of some of my transport animals. The joint caravan left Latooka on June 23 for Unyoro, Mrs. Baker in an improvised palanquin. The weather was wretched. Constant rains made progress slow; and the natives of the districts through which we passed were dying like flies from smallpox. When we at last reached Obbo we could proceed no further.

My wife and I were so ill with bilious fever that we could not assist each other; my horses, camels and donkeys all died. Flies by day, rats and innumerable bugs by night in the miserable hut where we were located, lions roaring through the dark, never-ending rains, made for many weary months of Obbo a prison about as disagreeable as could be imagined. Having purchased some oxen in lieu of horses and baggage animals, we at length were able to leave Obbo on January 5, 1864, passing through Farājoke, crossing the river Asua at an altitude of 2,875 feet above sea-level, and then on to Fatiko, the capital of the Shooa country, at an altitude of 3,877 feet.

III.—Discovery of the Nile's Sources

Shooa proved a land flowing with milk and honey. Provisions of every kind were abundant and cheap. The pure air invigorated Mrs. Baker and myself; and on January 18 we left Shooa for Unyoro, Kamrasi's country. On the 22nd we struck the Somerset River, or the Victoria White Nile, and crossed it at the Karuma Falls, marching thence to M'rooli, Kamrasi's capital, at the junction of the Kafoor River with the Somerset, which was reached on February 10. Here we were detained till February 21, with exasperating excuses for preventing us going further, and audacious demands from Kamrasi for everything that I had, including my last watch and my wife! We were surrounded by a great number of natives, and, as my suspicions of treachery appeared confirmed, I drew my revolver, resolved that if this was to be the end of the expedition it should also be the end of Kamrasi. I held the revolver within two feet of his chest, looked at him with undisguised contempt, and told him that if he dared to repeat the insult I would shoot him on the spot. My wife also made him a speech in Arabic (not a word of which he understood), with a countenance as amiable as the head of a Medusa. Altogether, the mise en scène utterly astonished him, and he let us go, furnishing us with a guide named Rabongo to take us to M'wootan N'zige, not Luta N'zige, as Speke had erroneously suggested. In crossing the Kafoor River on a bridge of floating weeds, Mrs. Baker had a sunstroke, fell through the weeds into deep water, and was rescued with great difficulty. For many days she remained in a deep torpor, and was carried on a litter while we marched through an awful broken country. The torpor was followed by brain fever, with its attendant horrors. The rain poured in torrents; and day after day we were forced to travel for want of provisions, as in the deserted villages there were no supplies. Sometimes in the forest we procured wild honey, and rarely I was able to shoot a few guinea-fowl. We reached a village one night following a day on which my wife had had violent convulsions. I laid her down on a litter within a hut, covered her with a Scotch plaid, and I fell upon my mat insensible, worn out with sorrow and fatigue. When I woke the next morning I found my wife breathing gently, the fever gone, the eyes calm. She was saved! The gratitude of that moment I will not attempt to describe.

On March 14 the day broke beautifully clear; and, having crossed a deep valley between the hills, we toiled op the opposite slope. I hurried to the summit. The glory of our prize burst suddenly upon me! There, like a sea of quicksilver, lay, far beneath, the grand expanse of water, a boundless sea horizon on the south and south-west, glittering in the noon-day sun; and on the west, fifty or sixty miles distant, blue mountains rose from the bosom of the lake to a height of 7,000 feet above its level. It is impossible to describe the triumph of that moment. Here was the reward for all our labour—for the years of tenacity with which we had toiled through Africa. England had won the sources of the Nile!

I was about 1,500 feet above the lake; and I looked down from the steep granite cliff upon those welcome waters, upon that vast reservoir which nourished Egypt, and brought fertility where all was wilderness, upon that great source so long hidden from mankind; that source of bounty and of blessing to millions of human beings; and, as one of the greatest objects in Nature, I determined to honour it with a great name. As an imperishable memorial of one loved and mourned by our gracious queen, and deplored by every Englishman, I called this great lake "The Albert N'yanza." The Victoria and the Albert Lakes are the two sources of the Nile.

IV.—Exploring the Great Lake

The zigzag path of the descent to the lake was so steep and dangerous that we were forced to leave our oxen with a guide, who was to take them to Magungo, and wait for our arrival. We commenced the descent of the steep pass on foot. I led the way, grasping a stout bamboo. My wife, in extreme weakness, tottered down the pass, supporting herself on my shoulder, and stopping to rest every twenty paces. After a toilsome descent of about two hours, weak with years of fever, but for the moment strengthened by success, we gained the level plain below the cliff. A walk of about a mile through flat sandy meadows of fine turf, interspersed with trees and bush, brought us to the water's edge. The waves were rolling upon a white pebbly beach. I rushed into the lake, and, thirsty with fatigue, with a heart full of gratitude, I drank deep from the sources of the Nile. Within a quarter of a mile of the lake was a fishing village named Vacovia, in which we now established ourselves.

At sunrise of the following morning I took the compass to the borders of the lake to survey the country. It was beautifully clear; and with a powerful telescope I could distinguish two large waterfalls that cleft the sides of the mountains like threads of silver. My wife, who had followed me so devotedly, stood by my side pale and exhausted—a wreck upon the shores of the great Albert Lake that we had so long striven to reach. No European foot had ever trod upon its sand, nor had the eyes of a white man ever scanned its vast expanse of water. We were the first; and this was the key to the great secret that even Julius Caesar yearned to unravel, but in vain!

Having procured two canoes, we started on a voyage of exploration northward on the lake. Along the east coast, with cliffs 1,500 feet in height, we discovered a waterfall of 1,000 feet drop, formed by the Kaiigiri River emptying itself in the lake. On shore there were many elephants, and in the lake hundreds of hippopotami and crocodiles. We made narrow escapes of shipwreck on several occasions; and on the thirteenth day of our voyage the lake contracted to between fifteen and twenty miles in width, but the canoe came into a perfect wilderness of aquatic vegetation. On the western shore was the kingdom of Malegga, and a chain of mountains 4,000 feet high, but decreasing in height towards the north. We reached the long-sought town of Magungo, and entered a channel, which we were informed was the embouchure of the Somerset River, from the Victoria N'yanza, the same river we had crossed at Karuma. Here we found our guide Rabonga and the riding oxen. The town and general level of the country was 500 feet above the water. A few miles to the north was a gap in the Malegga range; due N. E. the country was a dead flat; and as far as the eye could reach was an extent of bright green reeds marking the course of the Nile as it made its exit out of the lake. The natives refused most positively to take me down the Nile outlet on account of their dread of the Madi people on its banks. I determined, therefore, to go by canoe up the Somerset

River, and finally to fix the course of that stream as I had promised Speke to do.

V.—*Escape from Savage Enemies*

Both my wife and I were helpless with fever, and when we made our first halt at a village I had to be carried ashore on a litter, and my wife was so weak that she had to crawl on foot. At first the river was 500 yards wide, but on the second day it narrowed to 250 yards. As we pulled up the stream, it narrowed to 180 yards, and, rounding a corner, a magnificent sight burst suddenly upon us. On each side were beautifully wooded cliffs rising abruptly to a height of about 300 feet, and rushing through a gap which cleft the rock exactly before us, the river, contracted from a grand stream, was pent up in a narrow gorge of scarcely fifty yards in width. Roaring furiously through the rock-bound pass, it plunged in one leap of about 120 feet perpendicular into a dark abyss below. This was the greatest waterfall of the Nile; and in honour of the distinguished president of the

Royal Geographical Society, I named it the Murchison Falls.

Of course, we could proceed no farther by canoe, and landed at a deserted village. Our riding oxen had died; and we had to get some natives as porters. My wife was carried on a litter, and I was scarcely able to crawl; but after tremendous difficulties and dangers we reached, following the bank of the Somerset, on April 8, the island of Patooān, within eighteen miles of where we had first struck the river at Karuma. My exploration was, therefore, complete; but our difficulties were not at an end. We were detained for two months at Shooa Morū, practically deserted by everyone except our two personal attendants, and all but starved.

[The real Kamrasi, for the man Baker and his party had seen on their outward journey was only his brother M'Gambi, afterwards came on the scene, took them to Kisoona, and there and at other places detained them practically prisoners during the long and cruel wars with his rivals, Fawooka and Rionga and the King of Uganda. On November 17, Baker escaped with his wife and a small party and marched through the Shooa country and the country of the Madi to the Asua River, only a quarter of a mile from its junction with the Nile. Then they crossed the country of the Bari, and arrived at Gondokoro, whence they sailed down the Nile to Khartoum, which was reached on May 5, 1865, two years and five months after their start from that city.

The End